My Thoughts Were on America:
The Immigration of Isadore Flaschner

Edited by: Stephen S. Dashef, M D

JewishGen

מרכז עולמי לגנאלוגיה יהודית

The Global Home for Jewish Genealogy

A Publication of JewishGen, Inc.
Edmond J. Safra Plaza, 36 Battery Place, New York, NY 10280
646.494.2972 | info@JewishGen.org | www.jewishgen.org

MUSEUM OF JEWISH HERITAGE
A LIVING MEMORIAL
TO THE HOLOCAUST

My Thoughts Were on America:
The Immigration of Isadore Flaschner

Edited by Stephen S. Dashef, M D

Cover Design: Rachel Kolokoff Hopper

Library of Congress Control Number (LCCN): 2024931595

ISBN: 978-1-954176-93-5 (soft cover: 66 pages, alk. paper)

About JewishGen.org

JewishGen, an affiliate of the Museum of Jewish Heritage - A Living Memorial to the Holocaust, serves as the global home for Jewish genealogy.

Featuring unparalleled access to 30+ million records, it offers unique search tools, along with opportunities for researchers to connect with others who share similar interests. Award winning resources such as the Family Finder, Discussion Groups, and ViewMate, are relied upon by thousands each day.

In addition, JewishGen's extensive informational, educational and historical offerings, such as the Jewish Communities Database, Yizkor Book translations, InfoFiles, Family Tree of the Jewish People, and KehilaLinks, provide critical insights, first-hand accounts, and context about Jewish communal and familial life throughout the world.

Offered as a free resource, JewishGen.org has facilitated thousands of family connections and success stories, and is currently engaged in an intensive expansion effort that will bring many more records, tools, and resources to its collections.

Please visit https://www.jewishgen.org/ to learn more.

Executive Director: Avraham Groll

About JewishGen Press

JewishGen Press (formerly the Yizkor Books-in-Print Project) is the publishing division of JewishGen.org, and provides a venue for the publication of non-fiction books pertaining to Jewish genealogy, history, culture, and heritage.

In addition to the Yizkor Book category, publications in the Other Non-Fiction category include Shoah memoirs and research, genealogical research, collections of genealogical and historical materials, biographies, diaries and letters, studies of Jewish experience and cultural life in the past, academic theses, and other books of interest to the Jewish community.

Please visit https://www.jewishgen.org/Yizkor/ybip.html to learn more.

Director of JewishGen Press: Joel Alpert
Managing Editor - Jessica Feinstein
Publications Manager - Susan Rosin

Cover Photo Credits

Front Cover Photo: Post Card. *Polski: Pocztówka z początku.* J. Gelles, Public domain, via Wikimedia Commons
Front and Back Cover Background: Color and texture by Rachel Kolokoff Hopper
Front and Back Cover Background Photograph: *Winter's Grass* by Rachel Kolokoff Hopper

My Thoughts Were on America: The Immigration of Isadore Flaschner

Edited by Stephen S. Dashef, M D.

Preface

How did this book come into being?

When Grandpa Flaschner retired, except for the occasional garment he made for my family members, in the middle 1960's, my mother, his daughter, Selma Flaschner Dashef, thinking of ways to keep him busy, came up with the idea that he should write out the stories he told about his childhood. Mother typed his handwritten stories. I, then, wove the stories into a semblance of order.

Since Grandpa Isadore Flaschner spoke and wrote in several languages, I turned to Aaron Lansky of the Yiddish Book Center in Amherst Massachusetts who graciously helped me translate the Yiddish expressions which are italicized in Grandpa's memoir. These translations are in parentheses in the manuscript.

What kind of person was Grandpa Flaschner?

Grandpa Flaschner's pointing out things would sometimes anger me, but I knew he was concerned, like whether my shoes were shined or whether I had eaten each bit of food on my plate. He said earnestly that I deserved good clothes and an excellent education. As I grew, he announced to others that I was his bodyguard, then followed up with a statement about some recent accomplishment of mine. He was a short man with a pleasant smile, modest, devoted, and terribly hardworking. He had a gentle humor, evoked trust, and was very, very proud.

I remember being a toddler, living with my mother and grandparents, getting up at six in the morning, looking up from his feet as he explained how to cut oranges and squeeze them in a silver juice squeezer. The air was filled with orange aroma, care, and love. It only occurs to me now that he was standing in his own house, in his new land, with his newly purchased squeezer, preparing to go off to his own work. He possessed his present and created a future. I felt secure starting my day with him in the kitchen and looked forward to his return in the early evening, knowing that we would eat together as a family, and he would reliably say "good night" later.

His family and friends relied on him and esteemed him, too. He was a successful businessman, a raincoat manufacturer with his own factory and with dependable outlets for the distribution of his coats. His workers were loyal, for he was a staunch supporter of the union movement in the garment industry.

Grandpa Flaschner traveled the East Coast, gathering not only clients, but always searching out "new" family members as well. The family association he helped found grew to over four hundred members and for a time held annual meetings.

Since there was a sadness in looking back, he mostly looked

around himself and looked ahead. He was a caretaker of people and causes. Not orthodoxically religious, He believed in tradition and contributed financially to several synagogues. He made sure he attended every family event-- a bris, a Bar or Bat Mitzvah, a wedding, an anniversary.

Grandpa Flaschner socialized and played cards (mostly pinochle which he called poker) regularly with his friends. Treasuring his sense of family and community, he knew that he was fulfilling his own and his mother's dreams, determined not to live out the poor life with limited opportunity that was his father's life in his native Poland.

Mikulince, Galicia, the village in which Grandpa Flaschner was born and raised, is today (2013) in Ukraine. The spelling for Mikulince changes depending on the country in which it was located: Austria-Hungary, Poland, Germany, Russia. For a brief but detailed history of Mikulince including its spelling go to the following resource: https://myshtetl.org/ternoplskaja/mikulincy_en.html.

Grandpa Flaschner still had his sensitized awareness when I walked into his hospital room, having flown cross country to see him following his stroke in 1971. He could not move half of his body, felt degraded by this, and slurred his words, but nonetheless muttered out, "Did you bring Alysia?" (Alysia is my daughter.) He was slowly moving towards death, had not seen this great grandchild in two years, but was asking about her, never looking back, still moving his family into its future.

It seemed right that we buried him on a beautiful autumn day, with the sun out one more time as we moved across the countryside together.

Being thoughtful of other generations, he left these memories and thoughts for their sharing, especially with family and with friends. His voice speaks out to you in his declarative and straightforward way, with a mild Yiddish accent. If you listen well, you also hear a gentle and lyrical, sometimes sardonic, soul. He remembers his childhood and his rapid thrust into his precocious young adult years. This is a history of an adolescent boy moving from Poland to life in America in the first decade of the twentieth century. But it is also a piece of our national history, a revelation of the personal drive and energy behind the building of immigrant, industrial America, and, as such, his history, our history, is shared together here. He would be pleased to know that.

Grandpa's Memoir, in His Own Voice:

The whole city of Mikulince in Poland was in an uproar! Wherever one turned, whomever one met in the street, at the synagogue, in the marketplace, everywhere one went, the talk was about America. Young and old alike, except the incredibly old, who used to say that the sidewalks of America were treif. In Yiddish, the language Jews spoke to each other in Poland, treif meaning not kosher. The younger generation used to say the sidewalks might be treif, but the gelt, meaning money, was kosher. Day by day someone in town went off to the Golden Land, America. Raising money to get there was a problem, though.

Hardly anyone in Mikulince had enough money to start out for America on his own, especially a married person with children. How then did the pioneers of our town start to leave? To begin, you need to know about a man in town who was a Watty maker (he wove cotton batting used to stuff quilts). The Watty maker would loan money to people who pawned their candlesticks, pillows, and jewelry with him. He charged them interest, a real Shylock. This is how things worked: a man, wife and two children would pawn everything, or at least enough possessions for the head of the family to get to America. If the man was fortunate enough to get to New York and begin work, he then sent money home every month to pay off the loan. Whatever was left over after the monthly loan payments were made was kept by his wife and children in Mikulince for their own support. Each morning family members would run to the post office hoping

6

to find a letter with money from America.

This is the story of our Flaschner family's migration to America. The first to come was Uncle Samuel Flaschner, a young man about twenty-seven years of age at the time. He had served in the Austrian army, received an honorable discharge, and then married a girl named Chasa. Within a year or two, they became parents of a baby daughter named Sarah (now Mrs. Nasher of Golden Beach, Florida). Not having any trade, where was he to get money for his fare? It just happened that my father had married, and my mother had one hundred and fifty gulden as a dowry. Uncle borrowed this money with the promise he would send it back as soon as he had earned some money in America.

Well, to make this story short, he left Mikulince and after traveling a few weeks he went to Boston, Massachusetts, since there were a few *landsleit* (kinfolk) from home already settled there. The first thing he did though, once he earned some money in America, was to send a ticket and fare for his own wife and daughter. This was told to me by my mother in later years because her loan was never repaid. However, he did do other charitable deeds, taking the first step to see that family members left for America, one by one. First to leave after his wife and daughter was my father's sister, Esther Rifka.

There was soon no need to pawn more belongings for when they arrived on this continent, the women started earning about five or six dollars a week no matter what their line of work--in chocolate factories, blouse factories, or dress factories.

Men became peddlers, pressers, operators in the cloak shops, carpenters, painters, fruit peddlers, icemen, and whatnot. Soon, ticket agencies were opened in Boston's West End-- the Slobodkin agency on Lowell Street and Rothenberg's in the North End. These served as banks too. Every week people deposited what could be spared and then sent out steamship tickets and rail fare to cover the land trip from Mikulince to Hamburg, Germany, and to Rotterdam, Holland, and from these ports the boat trip to America. This early part of my story took place around the 1890's, when I was born. Esther Rifka, after a year or two, sent for her sister Sheindel (Jennie). Esther Rifka and Sheindel lived in Uncle Flaschner's house to start out and his home became "the station" for the family, all the *landsleit* from our city and surrounding towns being reunited there.

Before I tell you my own story, I want to introduce you first to Mikulince—the town and its people, their idiosyncrasies, and their lives.

This little city was about three quarters of a mile long, its width half a mile. The population was approximately five thousand: approximately one thousand Jews, approximately four thousand Gentiles. There were two stores in Mikulince that sold cloth. There were no retail clothing stores in the city since everything was custom made. The tradition was that when you got married, you had to make *auststafirung* (enough clothes) to last a lifetime.

The people that owned the cloth (fabric) stores were considered the rich class in town. There were about three grocery and butcher shops. There were two schools: the Baron Hirsch School for Jewish boys, and a public school for boys and girls. In my time school was compulsory and it started when a child was five and one-half years of age.

Mikulince had no water system, no sewers, no toilets, and no sanitary trucks. Sometimes in the summer the town had a few gentile street sweepers. For an entire year rubbish was thrown into a big pile that rose up to five or six feet high. When spring came, the town sent out a team and cleaned it away, using it for fertilizer on the fields. Since there were no sewers when it rained, the earth turned to mud, especially during the fall season.

So, the *blotter* (mud) can just be imagined! Shoes could not be worn, only *shtivel* (boots). People tied *honeches shmatys* (rags) around their feet instead of stockings. When they walked in the mud, the ground sounded like bubble gum popping. Outdoors, boards were used instead of sidewalks, or *stekkys*, (flat stones), were used like the flagstone patios here. Instead of walking one had to jump from one *stekky* to another. This mud lasted until *Pesach* (Passover, a spring holiday). In December, the snow started to fall; it was winter, and the snow never melted until after Purim. When you walked with boots a noise was made...skrip, skrip, skrip, skrip...regular music. The men put on their *tilip* (long coats with fur lining), tall fur hats and put both hands in their sleeves like the Chinese. Women wore heavy petticoats and heavy long shawls. The women that used to sell from stands in the market had fire pots with charcoal for heat.

Every small town had a market day on a different day. Mikulince had it on Monday, Strusuf on Tuesday, Tarnopol on Wednesday, Trembowla on Thursday. You still can find these cities on the map, when I authored this story, it was a part of Russia. On Friday, Saturday, and Sunday there was no market. Thursday night, most of the women were up all-night baking rye bread for the week and Challah bread for *Shabos*, the Sabbath. If one had children, one baked a little *koilitch* (challah) for each child. On Friday at 11 o'clock in the morning people ate a *podpalek* and *rossyl fleisch*. A *podpalek* is a piece of dough rolled like a pizza, about eight inches round, and baked before the bread comes out of the oven. It was a treat before the *Shabbos* meal. Sometimes one had *rossyl fleisch* (pot roast) with fresh bread from the oven also.

Since there were no toilets or restrooms in homes or buildings, little wooden sheds were built on the edge of the river. Each had a seat and two boards. One's feet were used to keep the door closed. These sheds were used by the men. The women ran early in the morning to the back of the *bud* (the Turkish bath) and wisely covered their heads with long shawls so as not to be recognized. In the daytime pigs cleaned the waste out. Dogs were on chains in town, but pigs ran around loose. The black crows would rest on the pigs' backs like bees on flowers. There were no slaughterhouses for pigs and every Gentile took care of his own.

In Mikulince almost everyone had a lengthy name, so nicknames were necessities. Hardly anyone could be recognized by his last, or family name. For instance, my father's name was Yekyl and his mother's name was Bessie. If people wanted to call him, they would say 'Y*ekyl Bessie's Zun.*' My friend, Sam Kutcher's father was Alter. If they wanted to call him, they would say *Alter Yidel Jankif Shmuel.* For Herman Friedman, people would say "*Hermann Nechi Chaim Kowal.*" This continued for generations until the younger folk started to go to school. Then they had to begin using family names. If your father had been married with a state license you could officially use your father's last name, but if you were married only by a rabbi in the Jewish faith, the wife was considered a common law wife, and the children would use their mother's maiden family name. That is how my cousin, Sam Flaschner, adopted his mother's name. His father's name was Greenberg. Of course, after the children finished school, most of them later used their father's name.

Let me tell you about some infamous town characters, known to all by their nicknames. Yankel was a man who had split his head in an accident and looked like he had two heads. Therefore, he was called "*Yankel mit sweikep*" ("Jacob with two heads"). Mordecai Boxer was renowned for having about ten wives, each of whom got sick and died. When one got sick, Mordecai would not call a doctor, but later he would say, "She died; now I know she must have been sick. "*Shmuel leib ich hab alein gesehed*" ("I really saw it"):

Shmuel was everybody's witness in court. The judge would ask him how it was that he became everybody's witness, and he would answer, "Believe me, your honor, I have seen it with my own eyes." Beryl Hipke Tunis was a con artist who sold rotten eggs, every Thursday, to a woman, Zisel Bella. A flat nosed Hebrew teacher, a *gonev* (phony or thief), he had come to Poland from Russia. Rosallie, the *Balabachte*, was the town fortune teller. She got hold of a woman peasant and would say, "Come, for five cents I'll guess your name...your name is Kathy." "Oh no," the woman would reply, "My name is Lapacinsky." "Oh yes," Rosallie would then say, "I made a mistake-—for that give me only two cents."

The *Balabachte* was also the one an illegitimate baby was brought to. She would manage to get rid of it. She also ran a general service agency. If anyone needed a servant, Rosallie would supply one. She supplied a wet nurse if a woman could not feed her newborn baby with breast milk, one who fed the baby for 25¢ a week. Balabachte was a fat woman, possibly 300 pounds. Her husband's name was Alter; he was skinny and small; his weight, I should say, was about 115 pounds. He was a *latutnik* (a reversible tailor). If anyone wore a coat or pants for ten years or more and wanted a new coat or pants, he brought it to Alter, who would rip the old garment apart and make it over on the reverse side. This became the new coat or pants. Sadly, the frail but resourceful

Alter ended up with TB and died.

Motel *der jusim* (Motel the orphan), was pitied by the whole city. Motel used to do the errands for everyone; he was always running around and busy. How Motel could have saved enough money to go to America remains a complete puzzle, but he did it.

Yitshok Poperek, four feet tall, married Yenty Leike, a very tall woman. Yenty, a poor relative of my grandmother, used to sell onions every Monday on market day. She put Yitskhok on one street corner selling his onions for a cent cheaper than her own so that all the peasants who came from the villages to the market kept him busy; when he sold out, she would immediately reduce her price. This was how they made their living. One-night Yitshok had a dream and started to yell, "*Yenty leike, ich bin ausgewachsen* " ("1 have grown"). This was dreamt on a Friday night and on the Sabbath, one must not light a match. So, the townspeople waited until Saturday morning and what a surprise they discovered. Yitshok was lying across the bed with his feet sticking out, so he was given the nickname *Poperek*, meaning sideways.

Godel *der Yayetchnik*, the egg man, to keep the eggs fresh, made a pool of lime or whitewash and threw the eggs in. They kept fresh for months. There were no iceboxes in Mikulince, but in the winter when the little river that ran through the town was frozen, the people would break the river ice and store it in the ground, 8 feet deep and 16 feet

13

wide. This ice could only be used as medicine. If anyone had a fever the local doctor would prescribe ice and with his prescription one could go to the Town Hall and chop off as much as was needed.

Mendel *der Melamid*, the Hebrew teacher, taught Gemara, higher learning in Hebrew. It was extremely hard to get Mendel pupils for he was a bad-tempered man. He had a lot of children; his wife gave him a child every year. On Thursdays, she would ask him for money for flour to bake bread for the week. Instead of giving money, he would beat her for asking. His wife was always black and blue, so no child wanted to learn in his *Cheder* (school). There was always a woman collecting bread or potatoes to bring into their home so they could eat and not starve, which was a constant danger.

Mikulince had a *burgermeister* (like a mayor), a Gentile doctor whose name was Brodzinsky, and a *weiss burgermeister* (an assistant mayor) whose name was Bomze, a Jew. The city had three police officers. It also had a Tax Collector and every man in town was required to pay a poll tax. The Town Hall was called the Gemeinde, and in it was also a police station. There were three churches: one Protestant, called Zerkwah; two Catholic, called Cloisters. They were lined up in a row. There was also one big synagogue and in the vestry of this synagogue there were small rooms which were occupied by tradesmen. The *schneider* (tailor) had a *schneider eske shulachyl* (little synagogue for tailors), the *schumacher* had a *schusterske shulachyl* (shoemaker's little synagogue) and the *trager* carrier (the wagon carrier) had his *shulachyl*.

There was a *Kipithince Claus* (room) so when der *Kipithince Rebby* came to town on a visit he would pray in his *claus*. There was a *Huriatymer claus*, and when the Rabbi from *Huratyner* came to town he prayed in his *claus*. They had their *Chasidim* (scholars) with them studying and *der rebby*, the rabbi, was reputed to be next to God. Then there was Chevra *Hanniti*, an organization made up of members who prepared the dead for burial.

The town had three wells that supplied the water to drink and water to cook with. Each family had a big barrel near its house and water carriers would fill up each barrel every morning at a cost of two cents a barrel. If a spider fell in the barrel of water, one had to dump the water out for it was said to be poisoned and the family was out of luck. There were fine kosher butcher stores called *Yatkis*. The rich men bought meat, while the poor families had bones, *kishke*, *miltz*, and *lungen* (lungs, intestines, pancreas, and other organs). There were also two tinsmiths in town, Yankel *der blecher* and Eli *der blecher*. Mikulince had two doctors, Dr. Brodzinsky, also the mayor, and Dr. Rosenbaum, a Jew. There were two barbers in town, as with the doctors a Jewish and a Gentile one. A barber was the person you would call if you had a stomach ache, and he would put *bankys* on your stomach. Bankys were little glass cups with alcohol in them. One merely lights a match and a cup stuck to your body for about one-half hour. The barber would put on twenty of these cups for ten cents. If you had a toothache, he could also pull a tooth. If you had a headache, he could put one or two leeches under your ear; they would draw blood, then the leeches would fall off. Jews never shaved, and rarely had haircuts, so the barbers needed to have this additional income from medical work. Only Gentiles in town shaved; there were no Gillette razors in Mikulince yet, so the barbers got this trade, too.

There were four tailors in town, one was Srul Eizik, a maker of cheap clothes, for men only. One was Ben Zion, the man I learned my tailoring from, who made officers' uniforms, priests' garbs, and rabbis' *bekyshys* (robes). Also, there was one ladies' tailor, lzyk Hersh. When a girl married, Hersh sewed clothes for her for the rest of her life. There was also *Froyim,* a common ladies' tailor; his work was not considered good at all. *Shwatchkis* were people who could make shirts. Most of the girls from the poorer classes upon reaching 13 or 14 years of age became *shwatchkis* and worked for two years for no money, just learning the trade. In Mikulince there was truly little money, so most of the girls became tailoresses. I will call them that.

There also was one *shamus* (a sexton). His duties included, on every Friday at about two o'clock, calling out at every two corners, "*In Shul arein,*" ("Go to synagogue"). He was like a town crier; his call was the signal for Jews to stop working and go to shul. When there was a death in town, the *shamus*, at five in the morning, would make two knocks on each Jewish door. That was a sign that somebody had died. Then there was *der Beder*, the man who owned the bathhouse; a few times during the month on weekdays he would have the bathhouse ready only for women. A *goy* named Yusky who owned a drum went all over the city yelling that the bathhouse was ready for the women. There was a *Soifer* (a scribe) in town that wrote the torah and after working hard all day on the parchment he went straight to the mikvah to dunk (take a ritual bath).

Mikulince also had a *schlachthaus* (slaughterhouse) where the *shocket* (an ordained religious Jew) killed chickens, ducks, and cattle. It was built on the little river which ran through the town. Ritual slaughter was performed by cutting the jugular vein. When a duck got loose after her throat was sliced, she might fly right into the river. The *goyim* (gentiles) used to stand in line after the cattle were killed and their skin pulled off to buy the hind, that part not being kosher, as sirloin steak. I remember with childhood awe how a cow would hang its feet up on these hooks, head down, and a knock over the head made it dizzy before the slaughter.

Most of the Jewish people were tradesmen, the balance were *meklas*, buyers and sellers. They went to the farms, buying anything they could possibly sell on market days. There were two *shadchens* (matchmakers) and they looked after marrying off poor orphan girls, to a *trager* carrier or a widower with children for instance. Just as long as the girls got married, they would make a living and then let God worry about the quality of the marriage itself. But, if a rich man had a daughter, the *shadchan* looked for *yichos* (upper class), what is called in America ``blue blood,'' men for mates. A scholar who married had to be given a dowry and a few years' kest (board and room); he must not work, just sit in a shul (synagogue) and study the *Talmud*. Before the wedding, a girl's hair was cut off and she wore a *sheitel* (wig). Such weddings began a week before the formal ceremony, with music played and the whole city coming out to drink. No matter where people lived, what part of the city, a ceremony was held outside of the synagogue, and there was a big town parade. Everyone in town ran to see it and after the ceremony, the guests, especially the Chasidim, danced like it was Simchas Torah as they approached the house of the bride. Yidel played his fiddle, and *Nute* (Nathan) played his bass and Yankel, the *trymaister,* his clarinet—you could hear the music a mile away.

Bertsie Flashner, the brother of Uncle Samuel Flaschner's, the patriarch of the family, was a blacksmith. He had a blacksmith shop, the only one in town. He ran related businesses too. People used to stand in line waiting for horses to be shorn. He also made the iron frames on the wheels for the wagons. He was very busy, and his three sons, Benny, Louis, and Nathan worked in the shop. Years later when they went to America, they established themselves in Newark, New Jersey, on Harvard Street, as blacksmiths, of course.

Uncle Lemuel was a baker. He baked all the matzah for Pesach. All the women in the neighborhood helped him stretch the dough and reel the holes, everything being done by hand. There was one drug store, the apothecary, which sold only medicine; there was no soda fountain. The scents of the various powders could be smelled blocks away. I remember my mother sending me there to pick up Solomian Tropper, a liquid to rub on the legs. I went and in order not to forget, 1 kept repeating the name Solomian Tropper time and time again, but when I got there, I forgot what 1 had come for. There were no telephones in Mikulince, so I had to return home empty handed.

There was a Mikulince brewery which made beer; whiskey could be sold by the government only. I used to go every Friday to buy a little bottle of whiskey for Kiddush and Havdalah. There was a *shenk* (a bar). They were really busy only on Mondays when all the goyim came to town for market day. What the farmers sold--chicken, eggs, and vegetables - and thus received money for, was quickly spent in the bar. The farmers went back home with much less money than they arrived with. Zallyl Stoller was a carpenter and made good income producing all the boxes for the market day. The *goyim* used to buy them to use as trunks also, and my father, himself a carpenter, helped him make them. The price: two *rammish* a box. Zallyl Stoller also used to make special coffins for the Jewish dead only, because the coffins had to be bottomless. By tradition Jewish people could not rest on boards, only on the bare ground.

In my day I, unlike my father's generation, began school because education was compulsory. Years before my time the Jews did not want to send their children to public school for fear they would grow up like *goyim*. At public school, all

19

children had to say *goyishe* (christian) prayers and had to cross themselves and that for Jews was a sin. Jews sent the boys to *Cheder* (Hebrew School) and the *rebby* taught them some arithmetic and if the child had a good head and parents could afford it, they would later send the boys to a *yeshiva*. But who could afford that luxury in Mikulince? The boys in town became tradesmen or started to sell and buy for the daily markets. Girls before my time grew up without knowing how to read or write Polish, German or Russian. However, if parents could afford a *Malamud* (teacher) to teach them *daven* (Hebrew prayers), the children then knew how to read the *siddur* (prayer book). On holidays in *shul* (synagogue) the women sat apart from the men. If one woman knew the siddur, a group of women who could not read and did not know what it was all about sat around that woman who could and listened to the reading of a *Tach charnysh* (a translated siddur like we have in America). Mostly though, the women cried and begged God that their husbands and children be well. Whatever came into their thoughts and lungs got cried out to the *RIBONO SHEL OILOM*--the Almighty God. As I reached 5 1/2 years of age, compulsory schooling became in fact a law, "a must" at that time. A wealthy Jewish philanthropist by the name of Baron Hirsch (Baron was a government title) established schools for Jewish boys only. No other religious group could enter the Baron Hirsch School. Girls had to go to public school. That too was necessary. Well, I was one of the first boys to enter.

The teachers were imported from Vienna, Austria, and from

Germany. One teacher was a local man whose father owned a brewery and he had gone to school in Leipzig, in Germany or Bavaria, and became a teacher. A lot of boys I knew started with me, Sam Kutcher, my best friend, Joe Tunis, Sam and Joseph Flashner, later from Philadelphia, and others. (Years later we all met in New York City, with my girlfriend, Annie. What a party we had getting together on Orchard Street at Chaim *leib, der shtricken dreir's,* the ropemaker's.) School opened with a prayer and a song in German, and we sang the national anthem. *"Gott erhalte, Gott beshitze, unser Kaiser, unser land"*..."God please take care of and protect our Kaiser and King Franz Joseph, and our land Austria, Hungary and Galicia." Then came the Hebrew anthem, *"Hatikvah'.*

We began learning languages in the first grade and by the third grade we already knew Polish and German. We had a particularly good scholastic system. Every hour we would have a different teacher on a different subject. When we entered, each boy received a suit, extra pants, shirts, handkerchiefs, boots--all part of a school uniform. At 12 o'clock, a woman and her Jewish help cooked kosher meals for the boys. Every week we had the same menu. On Monday, *Perel prop* (barley) beans and a piece of meat in the soup, three slices of bread and tea. Tuesday, *lochshen* (noodle) soup, a piece of meat, bread, and tea. Wednesday, *Kotleten* (cutlets), no soup, bread, and tea. Thursday *kasha* (groats) and milk, potatoes, and tea. Friday, no meals, since school was only a half-day because of the Sabbath. This continued week after week, with no changes. The suit and boots could be changed once every year when entering school. That was not a bad deal at all. Report cards were issued four times a year. Many boys did so well that they skipped grades. Dr. Landau was the Director of the school, Dr. Bonize, the Hebrew teacher. Dr. Lilker was a tough teacher whom none of the boys liked, for he used to punish the children. When he walked out of the classroom for a moment and returned to find the children talking, he ordered everyone to bend down and summarily whipped them with a *Kaushik*, a stick with leather straps. *Oy!* Did that hurt! You could not complain; there were no unions yet.

As soon as a report card was issued, I sent it immediately to my aunts, my father's sisters in America. I was allowed by my parents to do it, because when the relatives looked at it, they sent it back with a dollar or two. An American dollar was worth four in Galicia, a good deal for the family. I especially liked the month of May. We went every two weeks on *mayonikis*, hikes in the woods and had picnics. Our shoes or boots all had iron points so they did not wear out fast, and had metal horseshoes on the heels. And in the winter, we could skate on these heels sideways.

On a Friday morning in 1903, when I was about 10 years old, we were sitting in a school class, when the Director of our school suddenly called out, "Every one of you run home...don't stop...there is a fire next door... *es brent* (it is burning)." You can just imagine how we started to run. Most of the roofs in town were made of heavy straw and it happened to be a windy day. The sparks of the fire had

22

ignited hundreds of homes, smoke billowed up, and there was no fire apparatus. There were barrels of water, but they did no good. Men hand-carried pails of water and had to drop them on the fire. The heat was unbearable. People who could save some of their things if they had a team of horses, were the lucky ones. The old rabbi grabbed his *Sefer torah* and ran. My father tried to help us, putting some of our belongings in a trunk and carrying it away to the river, where he dropped it into the water. But the fire took care of the trunk too, which caught fire in the river. Hardly any homes were left. The little city was in ruins. And the smoke lasted for weeks. Help for food and clothing came from *landsleit* (kinfolk) in America and from the surrounding cities and towns. There were many people lost. Deaths were by the dozens. My mother was just out of bed from her delivery of my younger brother. I can remember that we barely made it up the very steep hill to a cloister built like a fortress with heavy stones and waited there for relief.

My mother's brother-in-law, named Fisch, in Tarnopol had two carriages. He sent these taxis down to Mikulince, picked us up and took us to Tarnopol to their house. The Fisches occupied two rooms and a kitchen. There was not enough room for all of us, so my father went to Hersh Tunis', Anna Tunis' father's house, and the rest of us stayed with the Fisch family. We were cramped there so my mother said to me, "I will borrow money and send you to Zborow to my sister, Taube; her family is very comfortable; they own a flour mill. Stay there until we can go back home.

I did not like the idea, but what could I do? They put me on the train and said good-bye. That was my first ride ever on a train. Finally, after what seemed ages of riding alone, stepping off the train, I asked where Bennie Fleishman, from the flour mill, lived. Some woman directed me, saying, "*Yingule dort voint er'*. "'Boychick (young boy), that is where he lives."

It was about five o'clock when I walked in. "*Guten abend tante!*" ("Good evening auntie"). She answered, "Good evening, *wus machst du*? (how are you?) How did you get here and where are your belongings?" I said I had nothing. They got burnt in the *feurer* (fire) and that mother had sent me here to stay.

"*Ny gut, hast shoin gedawent Minche?*" ("Well, good, have you already said your *Mincha* (afternoon) prayers?" "Yes, I did that on the train." 'Here, sit down, I will give you something to eat...How is your mother? I do not care much for your father. Can he make a living? You came here without anything at all! *Wei is mir* (woe is me). All right, you will go to sleep for the night. In the morning you must put on *tefillin* (prayer accessories) because you will soon be *bar mitzvah*. After that you will have breakfast, and then we will see what we can do for you. *Gott wet helfin* (God will help)."

Well, I did not entirely like the way I had been greeted, but what was I to say? I was like an orphan. That happened on a Thursday. I can still remember Friday morning, and how, when I woke up, I found my pants out in the hall. I decided that that was the end of my stay. I put on my *tefillin*, refused to eat, and cried that I wanted to go back to Tarnopol. They tried to encourage me to stay. "Nething doing," I said, "you can just give me carfare". I did not have a cent in my pocket. Finally, around 12 o'clock they gave me 50 cents. That was what it cost for a train ticket. I grabbed the money and ran to the train.

When I got to the station, before I even had time to look around to find where to buy the ticket, the train started moving. I jumped on and quickly went inside. Along came the conductor, "Tickets please~-no ticket, then it's *doulbed bezahling* (double price) while on the train." Well, I only had 50 cents. "Mo good...get off at the next station...buy a ticket there." The next stop was Yezernia, where my father used to go to visit the rebby on occasion. 1 got off, but before I could buy the necessary ticket, the train moved on and I was left at the station. First it entered my mind to go to the rebby. In the next thought 1 remembered that we had distant family in Yezernia, Ben Zion, a bookbinder; he had two daughters, Ethel and Rize. Rize was deaf and dumb, could not talk, but was smart as a whip. As I was standing and thinking, I saw some men and women, about ten of them, who asked me what had happened. I told them. Well, the same thing had just happened to them. They were actors and had to be in Tarnopol by eight o'clock for a show which they were putting on that evening. They asked if I had money. I said I had fifty cents. "Good," they said. "Give us the money; we are going to hire a team that will get us there." A *goy* with a big team of hay passed by. They stopped him. I do not remember what they paid him, maybe my full fifty cents, because that was a lot of money at the time. We all climbed onto the wagon. The wagon moved forward, and the group sang, talked, and acted. "Next year we are going to America," they said, "if we get the money for going." About eight o'clock we got into Tarnopol. When I saw the *Lemberger Gass*, Lemberg Street, I went off on my own and started to run because every house had their candles lit. It was already *Shabos*. God in heaven, I had sinned, I thought. My heart was beating rapidly. Running, I opened the door, then heard a yell from my mother, "*Oy wes mir* (Woe is me). What happened? How did you come back and why? You could have worked in the mill there. Now what is going to happen! *Nich gut*," (this is not good)." 1 said, "Mother, *Got wet helfin* (God will help)."

Mother went with me to another cousin, Goldsmith was his name, and I got a pair of green ladies' shoes. I fainted when I had to put them on. *"Oi gevalt"* ("Good heavens"). I do not remember where she got me a pair of pants. Anyhow I came into the store at nine o'clock in the morning. The boss looked me over, called over the clerk or salesperson and told him, "This boy is a fire refugee from Mikulince. Treat him well. Tell him what to do. I am sure he will do decent work. I know his uncle. Give him proper instructions. I am going away for two days. You report to me on how he's done when I get back." Here were the instructions for my first job: 'When you get in in the morning, take a broom and sweep the sidewalk as clean as a whistle. Then take a brush and brush all the piece goods that are on the shelves. Dust the skins, placing beaver on beaver, *persian* (lamb) on *persian*. Be careful with the sealskin, that is expensive. And, when all is finished, sweep the floor and mop it with *pollistur* (wax). Then, go out for coffee. When you come back, I will go to eat. These tasks take me two hours. If a customer comes in while I am gone, talk to him until I come back. Do not leave him alone in the store. If anyone brings you money, take it. If anyone wants money, tell him to wait until I come back myself," I would run over to the Goldsmith's for my coffee. The Goldsmiths drank the real coffee; they gave me chicory instead, with a slice of black bread with *shmaltz* (chicken fat) and that was all. After two days the boss returned. He had bought new skins at bargain prices at the Lashkowitz Fair. When the team brought in the merchandise, I was the one to sort them. The salesman gave him a good report on me, and the boss said, "Now you are going to get 50 cents a week for your work, and you'll have supper in our home every day."

The first day I was there the family sent me out to buy *shinke* (ham} and knockwurst. "Well," I thought, "if they ever give that to me, I'll be committing a sin...the ham is *treif* (not kosher)." I brought the food up to them and they let me keep the change. That supper consisted of bread, mashed potatoes, a little wine, and tea. And so, every day I had my supper with them. The food was tasty, whatever they prepared. The family even had servants. I enjoyed the situation there so much that I gave up going to the Goldsmith's for coffee.

One morning when I came into the store, the clerk again told me that the boss would not be in for two days, so I routinely started to do my work. Suddenly, the clerk told me to take the cardboard out from the rolls of cloth. I started to unroll the cloth, taking out the boards, as many as 1 could. He said, "There is a bookbinder on the Lemberger *Gass*. Go in there and sell the boards to him. I need the money." I did what he said, since he was in charge, and gave him the money. Two days later the boss arrived home with a lot of cloth and remnants and said, "Itzoch Abe, assort them for me and place them on the shelves." His eyes then spotted that the cloth on the shelves had no boards. "Where are the boards?" he asked. The clerk pointed to me, "He sold them." *Oy gevalt* ("Oh my God")," I yelled, "what a *liger* (liar). He himself told me to do it, and I brought and gave him the money." The boss paused before he spoke. "If this is so, and I believe you, well I'll pay him off and it's good riddance." The clerk summarily left, and I was left with the responsibility to open the store and to close it up. The windows and doors had metal rolling gates which closed tightly. Furs and cloth were expensive and to prevent thefts by burglars, the owners had their place secured.

Unfortunately, I could not stay for long, because my folks wanted to get back to Mikulince to see what to do with the remains of our burnt-out house.

So sooner than I had wished I had to give notice that I was leaving. The boss felt sorry, too, since I could become a clerk when I got older. He gave me a few yards of navy pencil stripe material for a suit. That cloth became the first suit a tailor ever made for me, in Tarnopol. I left home as a boy and came back as a real sport. Once back in Mikulince, my mother rented an alcove for the four of us at Leibush's, the *trager* carrier's (the mover's). (If there was anything anybody had to send or something heavy to move, Leibush was the transporter.) Leibush, his wife and his daughter, who was my age, shared a front room. There was a lot of talking by the adults about how his daughter and I would be a good match after we grew up, and of course after I had learned a trade. First, I would learn to be a tailor, and she would learn to be a *shwatchka*. (A *shwatchka* makes shirts, aprons, underwear.) Those were their thoughts. But my *head* was on America.

As I was now getting a little older, and with pressure coming from my aunts in Boston, my folks decided for me that there had to be a *tachlis*. That is to say, I must have a future. Higher schooling was out of the question in Mikulince. And who could send me to Tarnopol for school? Where would they get the money? No, that was out, too. Now what was I going to be, a *stoller* (carpenter)? That was my father's work, and it was too hard a life. A shoemaker? No. In America, tailors take in gold, so the choice must be a tailor. America was always being kept in mind, so on a certain Saturday night, a night of the Chanukah festival, we went to Ben Zion, the best *schneider* (tailor) in Mikulince. We came in and said, "*Ein gute woch* (a good week), Reb Ben Zion; we have decided to make our son, Yizchok Abe (Isadore Abraham), into *ein schneider* (a tailor) and only with you." Ben Zion contemplated the proposal, "All right," Ben Zion said, "Three *Yahr* (three years) and you have to pay ten *ranish* every year. If he proves to be good, I will not demand the last ten *ranish* (dollars). He has to be here at seven in the morning and he'll go home after I finish *Maariv* (night prayers}." Well, that was it; it was settled. School ended in May, and I began immediately after school ended.

The instructions from my first day at work come back to me even now. "Number one: As soon as you come in, you must see that this work room is clean. Sweep it. When I come in I will show you how to thread a needle. You must get a thimble, take a piece of cloth, hold the thimble this way and make believe you are sewing. This you must do for one month. After that 1 will show you more. Do not go near the sewing machine." At that time, the Singer Company had produced a machine like the 31-15 but with a big head, and to run it one had to put both feet on two iron pedals which fitted the soles of the shoes. You had to go back and forth with your feet for the wheel to turn. It took four months before I was allowed to get near Ben Zion's machine.

During this period, a garment for the Protestant priest was finished and I was the one designated to bring it to him. Shivering I went; he was a *Galach* (Galach is the word for priest in Yiddish) and I was afraid. I shivered because of the legends I had grown up with, that *Galachs* caught Jewish children and put them in a cloister until they converted to Christianity. Well, I delivered the garment and to my surprise the priest spoke to me in Yiddish, telling me stories and treating me to a glass of tea. After spending a little time with him I left. I was in a hurry to get back since it was

Friday afternoon. It would soon be sundown, the *Shabbat* {Sabbath). He gave me a tip of a *krone* (50 cents). This made me feel as if I had become a money earner, since I hardly got anything from my father and my mother never had any money to give. My master, Ben Zion, never gave me as much as a penny candy.

Meanwhile 1 had to do all the family errands. "Go to the *yatki* (butcher shop) and get me good meat", was the order from Mrs. Ben Zion. 'Be careful to get good meat, for if the meat is not, you will only bring it back...Be sure to run because when you get back you must take out the *pomnis* (water) to wash all the children (nine of them besides themselves). Make it fast, the day is pretty near gone." This happened day in and day out. At night, when I went home, I had to report on how far I had advanced. Well, I advised my mother that I did not want to be a *schneiderer* (tailor); I wanted to be a *katzef* (butcher). I already knew about *flanken*, *ling* and *leber* (lung and liver), chuck, a *shtikel kisky* (a little stuffed derma) and so on. My mother was stunned. The next Saturday night my mother went to Ben Zion. She said, as she had in the past, "*Ein gute woch* (a good week). Tell me *Herr* (Mister) Ben Zion, *vus vet sein der tachlis* (what will happen in the future)?" But then she added, "You want to make my boy into *ein shick yingel* (errand boy)?"

Ben Zion was taken aback but replied, "Don't worry, Esther, we have a long time yet, I assure you that when the three years end, he will be a good tailor. I can see he has a good head, and he likes to work. He does everything I tell him.

31

Good night; come some other time when I'm feeling better."

The next day, I did no errands. The master cut a few pants and I started to sew. Not on the machine, but by hand. In order not to ravel the garment I had to *merrow* (overstitch) the edge. Today there are *merrow* machines but not in my day. Well, since I no longer did errands, I sat on one chair from early morning 'til supper time, with the exception of going home to eat. Meanwhile, while 1 worked, the boss took a nap for a few hours. I had to wait until he awakened to be given permission to go home. That routine went on for a few months; finally, he allowed me to try to sew on the machine, making cotton pants for the peasants, and when the year was over, I was able to make a pair by myself.

But the family had to scrape together the ten *ranish* as per our contract. Somehow, with a little help from my aunts in America, we got the money. My Mother went to Ben Zion with the money and told him, here is the ranish. "Be a good man," Mr. Ben Zion, and teach Yizchok Abe to make a *vestaly* (vest)." "Yes," he said. "First he has to learn to make a good pair of pants from *serge* (heavy woolen cloth) and that's hard. Then we will see *veiter* (further)." My mother left. The next day the first thing he told me was that my mother was a smart woman. She wanted too much; she could be an *advocat* (lawyer). I was to keep quiet and wait.

It happened one day that the Barnum and Bailey Circus came to Tarnopol, and the master left to see it. His wife and children were at home. Unexpectedly a woman came in. Her husband had died, and she needed a black suit for his burial right away. The Mrs. Boss came in and said, "Yizchok Abe, do you think you can make a suit? After all, you have been here for over a year.' To say no would mean that my progress would be held back, so I said yes. "It has to be done in two days." When I went home for supper, I was given the courage to go back, told to cut it, to make it bigger than the man, with no pockets of any kind. The man was dead anyhow. Even if I had to stay all night, I was to show Ben Zion what I could do, then he would have to give me a start on a vest and maybe a coat also. Well, I went to work, using no patterns. I took a jacket that was hanging up half-made, chalked' cut every part, gave the man plenty of room, cut the pants big like a clown, and got busy working all night. When Mrs. Ben Zion came into the workroom the next morning, the suit was pressed. She was quite pleased and offered me breakfast. I had become one of the family. All the neighbors soon knew what I had done. The next day I had an offer from the boss that if I wanted to work on Saturday night after *Maariv* (evening prayers), I could have *chal a shudis* (an evening meal) with them. They left it for me to decide. Now I knew that they needed me too and I could be more independent. I worked hard. 1 wanted to get somewhere. America was on my mind. The days went fast, with no rest or exercise except on Saturdays. Gradually the second year passed. I already had made a good pair of pants. In three and a half hours I made a pair of pants and a vest, but not a coat. One Friday at one o'clock, after finishing my work, Ben Zion said to me, "Tell your father to come over, I have some important matter to take up with him. Tell him to come on

Shabbos after *Maariv*." I went home with the message wondering what he could want. Maybe he wanted the ten *ranish* again. If so, where would I get it? *Gott veist* (God knows). My mother said, "So what? 1f he will not teach him anymore, Itzchok Abe can get a job with someone else. Don't worry, *Gott vet helfen* (God will help)." On Saturday night, my father and my mother came down to meet the boss. The talks started. "I want to tell you something special. As you know, Jekyll, you are to pay me ten more *ranish* and I know you might be cramped for money. I will let it go and I also will give your son three meals a day. He is exceptionally good at his work, and he will become a craftsman soon. He will make a complete garment beginning on Sunday. Another boy is coming in to learn to be a tailor, also.

By the end of my apprenticeship, I had made a coat and a *bekishe* (a robe that the rabbi's wear), and also helped work on uniforms and priestly garbs. I began receiving job proposals, one being that as soon as I finished my apprenticeship, I could get a job paying ten *cronen* a week. That was five *gulden* (four *gulden* or one *ranish* was one American dollar). All these proposals went through my agent, my father, not being made directly to me.

Well, the day finally came and on Chanukah my father went over to Ben Zion's to tell him my time was up. I had to get a certificate since I had finished my apprenticeship. If Ben Zion wanted me to work for him, I would now have to be paid. Ben Zion told me to come in tomorrow and he would see about it.

The next day I went over but refused to sit down unless I received my certificate. He started laughing and began telling a story. 'You know, Itzchok Abe, during the three years you must have been sick at times. You also stuck a needle in your finger, and you were out of work, in Tarnopol, at the workmen's clinic for a few weeks. Therefore, you must remain here for another year, or at least six months. This is what I have decided, and you can start right now." I said that I was going home. Coming home with the news, my mother replied, "Go back and tell him you will give him three months of work, from Chanukah until Purim, and no more." I went back with her message. As I entered his shop, he asked what they had said. I told him that my mother had said from Chanukah to Purim. "Oh, your mother is too smart, let it be from Purim to *Shavuath*." I returned home with his message and the fun began.

The next morning my mother and I went to the Director of Schools. I can remember distinctly how she was greeted, "Itzchok Abe's Mama, what can I do for you?" She told him the whole story. He sat down and wrote a letter to the city *advocat* (attorney) asking him to help me get what was coming to me from Ben Zion or else he would take Ben Zion to court. Ben Zion ignored the attorney's letter. Next came a summons to court. The attorney already had conferred with the Judge. Then the attorney called for my mother by a messenger, there being no telephones in Mikulince. She was advised to go to court and to tell the Judge at trial what had happened.

Well, a day before the trial, my mother sent a pound of butter to the Judge's wife, and Sam Kutcher served as my witness to the transaction that had previously happened. The next day in court the Judge asked Ben Zion why he refused my certification. Ben Zion started to tell all kinds of stories, then my mother told her version. The Judge made an immediate decision, a two hundred dollar fine to be paid in twenty-four hours by Ben Zion or go to jail. The Judge also sent out a messenger to an old tailor in town telling him to try me out for ten days. After ten days I was awarded my diploma by court verdict, and I went to work for Issac Miller for ten *Kronen* a week. Friday noon each week was payday, and my father would send my older brother Sam over for the money. Out of it I got my allowance of 50 cents for the week.

It was the only payment I would receive because I was getting ready to leave for America.

Ben Zion paid the fine and the whole town knew what had happened. Wherever he went, people teased him. One Saturday sometime later at the *shul* (synagogue) a fight started between my father and Ben Zion. Well, I was not there because I was already on the way to America, so I cannot tell you who won. But years later, when I was married and living in Stoughton, Massachusetts, in America, this same Ben Zion found his way there. My wife and I accepted him as a visitor yet then he announced, "You know what I came for? I want my two hundred dollars, which I paid for the fine." This he did not get, for two hundred dollars in 1913 was a lot of money in Stoughton just as it had been in Mikulince. Ben Zion left for New York, where I understand he passed away.

To back up just a bit, it was after my Bar Mitzvah and near the end of my training that I began thinking actively of plans for going to America. In school and with boyfriends we talked mainly about America, how wonderful it was there. Every boy sought an uncle or cousin to whom he could write for help to leave for the new country. Some who had no relatives in America started out by walking to Germany, to France, or to London to try and better themselves. Finally, my turn had come. I sat down and wrote a letter to my aunts, Esther Rifka and Shaindel, who were now married. Esther Rifka had married Max Rosenberg, a butcher, and Shaindel married Dave Appel, a "Columbus" tailor. A Columbus tailor was one taught in America--a "fly by nighter". As long as a man could master the sewing machine, he was called an "operator"-- a cloak operator or skirt operator or blouse operator. This is the letter that I wrote and sent out:

Liebe Tantes and Uncles: (Dear Aunts and Uncles:)

You know that I have finished my academic grades in school for I sent you my report cards every year. Now I am about to finish the three-year apprenticeship at the tailors.

This is what you wanted me to do. You wrote to my mother when you arrived in America, "Tailors in America shovel gold in the streets "*mit a lopaty*" ("with a wooden shovel").

Now that I am finishing my apprenticeship, I would ask you to please send me a *Shifskarte* (boat ticket), and *resse shpezen* (car fare to the boat), and when I come to your America, I will repay you every cent. I will also be able to help my father and mother and will send for my brother when he grows up.

I had a tough time getting money for a stamp to mail the letter. Finally, my mother, after reading my plea to go to America and to be able to help her, sent the letter. It took weeks to receive a reply. Meanwhile, I watched expectantly for the letter carrier every day and would sing the same song, "Have you a letter for Yekel Flaschner from America?" (We had to write Yekel Flaschner to distinguish our family from another Jacob Flaschner, the father of Joe and Sam of Philadelphia. The mail carrier used to deliver our mail to their house. Due to the trouble and confusion we decided to use the original name Yekl and the other changed his name to Jankel. In that way the problem was settled once and for all. Well, the day finally came; there was a letter from America.

Lieber Bruder und Schwägerin Esther:
(My mother's name was also Esther.)

Dein Sohn Izyk Abe's letter erhalten. Er schrieb

einen guten brief. (He writes a good letter.)

A railroad ticket and boat ticket will be sent to him as soon as he finishes his three-year apprenticeship. We are going to deposit money in Rothenberg's Ticket Agency, and it will be there just in time for his departure to America.

At this same time, my boy friends, Sam Kutcher and Moshe Yanover (Moshe's real name was Lederman but his father came from a city named Yanover, so they had changed his family name to Yanover), and I started writing letters to an agency in Germany and one in Holland for information about the cost of transportation to America. The first letter 1 wrote read this way, with the address first:

I. Missler Bremen Banhoff Strasse No. 30
Bitte mir einen Presscorant zuschicken, weil ich nach Amerika fahren will.

Sighnen
Izyk Abe Flaschner

Kindly send a brochure and prices since I want to go to America.

Isadore Abraham Flaschner

In a few days I received an answer with a catalog and pictures of boats on the Holland America Line N.A.S.M.

This was my happiest moment. For now, I knew the cost of passage just in case my aunts did not send me a ticket, so, if necessary, when I finished my training, I would just save my money and buy it myself.

My mother and father were not happy with my plans. How could they allow a boy of thirteen or fourteen to go into the big world by himself? Naturally, they started to cry, especially my mother, "No," I was told, "at least not for another few years."

Meanwhile, my mother got in the family way and had a difficult delivery. She had another boy, her third, and they named him Vigdor. One of their friends had passed away and no one had been named for him as yet, so for the receipt of five krone they named the baby after the friend.

Around this juncture, my father decided he was going to go to America first and wrote to Uncle Flaschner requesting a ticket for the money which Uncle owed him. After a while father got an answer saying, "America is not for you; you're better off staying home." He then wrote to his sisters, being their only brother, and they replied differently, that they thought he could do well in America. The ticket, which they also sent to him came along with twenty Gulden, carfare to the boat in Hamburg. You can just imagine what happened then in our home. Everybody in the house was crying; my mother was not well; money was low. "Crying won't help. Trust in God, Father said.

He made plans to leave that Sunday for Tarnopol to get the train. He would take under his care a boy of eleven years, Chaim Galner; Chaim's father, in Boston had sent for him. Chaim's mother would help our family with money to live until my father got to America. Then father would send us money to live on until he could take us all over to America. Father said good-bye, and no sooner had he left than my mother, brother, and I started crying without stopping. The young Vigdor did not understand what had happened. Five days elapsed. One night we received a telegram saying, "Send me money, I was turned back." No reason was given. Mother started to yell, "*Gewald Gott* (Dear God), what can I do! Where shall I get money? We don't have a cent in the house." I said, "Mama take the pillows, wake up the cotton maker and pawn the pillows and the feather bed." I helped her carry them to him, but we had a hell of a time getting the loan. We were hysterical and nearly fainted before he finally gave us twenty *Kronen* and we telegraphed the money to my father. Five days later, amidst great disappointment, he came home. The reason he was turned back I do not know even to this day. (Father lived well into his eighties and perished in the Holocaust.) Chaim Galner was taken from him and sent to Boston with Travelers Aid, a sign pinned on his back and front. The sign read, "GOING TO MY FATHER IN AMERICA."

This was my father's first and last attempted trip. He sent back the ticket to his sisters, who had to take a loss both on the money for carfare and a few dollars on the ticket itself. Meanwhile time had marched on. My time as an apprentice expired and I was getting ready for my diploma. 1 wrote to my aunts for a *Shiffskarte* and in a few months I received it along with carfare. Now I needed a passport so that I could pass through all the *grenetz* (borders) from one country to another until I reached Rotterdam, Holland. How was I to get this passport? I had to go to the *Gubernator* (Governor), but my parents could not even give me the carfare to Tarnopol. My mother said to me, "You know what? Go to Shabsy Masters, (His sons became Doctors Harry and Joseph Masters of Revere, Massachusetts.) He is going with his cattle to Tarnopol to the market *yarid* (place). You will walk along slowly with him and act like a man. Go up to the Governor's office and get the passport. You will get it and it will not cost anything. You are not of age yet to serve in the army." (By the way, Shabsy's wife was my mother's stepsister——one mother but not one father, a partnership business.)

Well, I took my mother up on her proposition. What else could I do? Shabsy Masters said yes, I could walk with him. So, one night he started out with about fifty cows on a long, muddy road. The cows walked in a line. He walked with a whip behind them, and I followed him. It was only three miles from Mikulince to Tarnopol, but European miles are much longer than American ones. Finally, in the morning we got to the *shrank* (tollhouse) and paid two cents a cow and one cent a person. After passing through the gate,

I took a walk to see my mother's sister, Yetta Fish. (At the time, Ben, her son, was a boy of my age. He became a doctor years later.) Yetta made me put on *Tefillin* and say prayers, then fed me breakfast of bread, salt, onion, potatoes, and water. After I finished eating, I went off for my passport. My heart was beating quickly, and I said good-bye. There I was at the door of the large public building. I walked into one of the rooms and sat down. A man came over and spoke Polish, asking what I had come for. I told him I was there to get a passport to America, explaining each of the countries I had to pass through on the trip. I had my birth certificate with me, as well as my school diploma and my hard-earned apprentice diploma. He looked at everything and asked if I would come back to serve in the army. I said I would do that, and he stamped a passport and gave it to me. Suddenly I felt enormously relieved. I took it, thanked him, and kissed his hand, and put it in my pocket.

I made certain I would not lose it and out I ran, straight for Mikulince, alone, shaking in my boots. 1 was afraid of the *goyim* (Christians), who used to throw stones at Jews, and knew that during the three miles I had to pass through four towns and villages. There was an inn along the way which a Jewish fellow ran and all the teams that went by stopped there for a snack or a drink.

Since I had my passport, I felt like a big man and went there for a rest. The man of the place came over, gave me his hand, and offered a "*shalom.* He asked if I had said my morning prayers and offered me a cup of *kawa* (coffee). After a brief rest I was on my way home. I did not walk. 1 ran most of the way, motivated with both fright and happiness. Finally, I arrived home but it was already dark. 1 came into the house tired. "*Oy wei*," cried my mother. "First eat and then you'll tell me all about the passport." She fed me the basics--borscht, potato, black bread, and tea——and when I was finished, she asked, "Now tell me, did you see *Mimy Ettie* (Aunt Yetta)? How is she? And Uncle Moishe? And what about your passport? Will you have to return there again?" I answered that I had it and did not have to go again. Now I would have to get ready to leave. "Good," she said, "Now we have to go to the *rebby* (rabbi) for a *Brucha* (a blessing) and we have to get a suitcase and I am going to bake *sucharis* (dry toast), plenty of them. You will not be hungry when you go by train from Tarnopol to Lemberg. When you come to Lemberg, knockwurst will be sold on the platform; buy one. I am going to sew your carfare into your vest pocket. Keep some change to spend and be certain if you cannot carry the suitcase to get a porter and give him *tringelt* (a tip).

He will take you where you must go..." This type of talk lasted for weeks, for they hated to see me go alone despite my being able to speak German, Polish, Russian, Ukraine and Yiddish. Meanwhile, everyone in Mikulince got to know that Izyk Abe, Yekil Stolarz's (the carpenter's) son, was going to America. Every night people that had family or friends in New York, Boston, or Philadelphia (for Polish people, there was no California or Florida in those days) came to our house. There was one song that was sung——"give my father, brother, or sister *eingriiss* (regards) and tell them to send me money or a ticket...do not forget...*fershreib* (write it down) ..." Most people in town had the idea that only New York was America!

My Trip to America

The time to leave drew nearer and nearer. The house turned gloomy. Tears streamed from everybody's eyes including my own. 1 am leaving. God knows whether I will see Father and Mother again. A shiver went through my body. This all happened on *Pesach* (Passover) in April, my fourteenth birthday, and I decided to leave home on June 17th, 1907. All my boyfriends and girlfriends came over to the house to wish me good luck...'we will see you in America sooner or later." I was the first of my friends to leave. My entire fortune consisted of the boat ticket and twenty *Kronen* for railroad fare, three *Kronen* for spending money and tips, the suit that I wore, and a satchel with a shirt, underwear, pajamas, pants, and of course the dry toast, an orange if I got sick, one apple, one pear and the passport. Oh, also a comb and a brush to clean my cotton suit that I wore. I still have this brush today and someday I will give it to one of my grandchildren who will promise to keep it as a remembrance. This brush was my mother's present from her grandmother when she was a little girl. She also gave me two *proskys* of china filled with a type of aspirin for headaches, in powder form. Everything was set. A neighbor came in to say that his daughter Goldie was also going to New York on the seventeenth of June and suggested that we go together, for Goldie was much older than I, and twice as big, a real lady. Feeling relieved, my mother cautioned Goldie to be sure not to leave me, to take diligent care of me, and God would then help her make a good *zywyk* (match) in which she would be happy.

A team was hired to take us to Tarnopol where we started out by train to Lemberg, the capital of Galicia. Finally, the 16th of June arrived and, my Lord, the whole town came to say goodbye. My mother was in the throes of tears all day. My father held my mother. My brother, Sam, kept crying. My brother Vigdor who was close to three years old passed away shortly thereafter. (I still remember him, a husky boy. He had an excessively big head.)

He had gotten sick and in a few days he rapidly died.) Despite our grief, along came the 17th, six o'clock in the morning, and the team was at the house. Yankel der Kirshner's (the furrier, who had a nickname Maginot, rich) daughter Goldie and I placed our suitcases into the wagon, and it started moving forward, all of us walking along slowly beside. My mother's words, the last words of hers that I ever heard, were, "*Itzik Abenue (Isadore Abraham) gedenk die solst shreiben*...Remember, you should write, and you should keep Esther Rifke (my father's sister) as your mother.

I do not think I will ever see you again. Promise me that you will never smoke. You nearly lost your father through his smoking." 1 answered, "I promise," and that was the end.

We walked quite a long way together, about half a mile, and the team stopped. We hugged and cried, then I got into the wagon. They all turned back, and we were on our way to Tarnopol at eleven in the morning. Once we reached the gate of the city, we had time to wait for the train until three o'clock in the afternoon, so I went to visit my mother's three sisters, Etty, Lany, and Hindy. They lived near each other. After saying good-bye, I went along to *Rebby* Reb Kopaly's. His name was Koppel but a rabbi is always spoken about affectionately--Kopaly, Hershaly, Zudikl, Beraily--because each has his admirers. The *Rebby* knew me because my father had been his *chussid* (student), having spent holy days with him. He blessed me and gave me a cameo, a penny, with the admonition that when I crossed the Atlantic Ocean, 1 was to throw it in the water and not to forget him and I would then be a happy man all my life.

Next it was on to the train! Coming to the station, in the big waiting room, we found a lot of people going to America. The Traveler's Aid and Boat Agency had their men in all the big stations aiding passengers and directing them about which trains to take, advising both those with passports and those without how to reach their destination. Goldie kept an eye on me, she did not let me move a step from her. Finally, we were on the train, moving slowly at first, then faster and faster, going and going, away and towards. She kept my train ticket in her valet so I would not lose it. We did not eat that night; we only thought about how our parents must have been feeling at home. We seemed so far away. On the morning of the 18th, we arrived at Lemberg, a big station with a noticeably big platform where men sold beer and knockwurst. We each bought a wurst and drank beer. The committee was waiting for us, and took us into another car headed for Krakow, the main capital of Galicia. This trip took a day and a night. Next, we traveled into Austria, I think it was to Vienna, and then we were to go to Berlin, Germany. We found it easy to pass through everywhere. Only those boys that had to serve in the armies found it difficult; they had to *shmear* (tip) the agents to get through. Finally, we entered Berlin, Germany, not leaving the train there. Additional cars were hooked on for the trips to France or Holland. From Tarnopol it took five days all told to get to the boat, either in Amsterdam or Rotterdam. After a very tiring five days we reached our destination. We were taken in various quarters, like cattle.

Some of the women with children lost their husbands along the way. Being without funds, they often had to steal to pay their way from one country to another to get to the boat. So, these women kept on waiting, some waited for days. It was a pity to see the anguish they went through. We slept on the station floor for two nights waiting for the boats to leave.

In Rotterdam I parted from Goldie - she went on one boat, I on another. My boat was the Statendam. It was a relief at last to get into the stateroom. Since the room was third class, it had three bunks. I slept on the top bunk and two elderly people slept on the first and second bunks. Everyone came from a different country--from Poland, Russia, Romania, Lithuania, Kurland, Galicia, Austria and many more—-most of them Jews. I had never been in the majority before. First and second-class passengers enjoyed good meals, but the third-class passengers got the leftovers. But as they say "*Kol Yisrael Chaverim"* ("All Jews are brothers and friends"). The first and second class had enough of their own food, so they did not forget me. I was fed. We said our prayers morning, noon and night, and all day long Jewish and Hebrew songs were sung. It was a closeness to remember. I was a skinny little fellow, very dark, with a short haircut and with sideburns, not too long, but long enough to make me look attractive. There were two passengers on the boat, good looking women in their twenties, who came down from upstairs (first or second class) to listen to Jews sing their songs - *Shema Koleim, Yakin Pirkon min Shmayon Askinaim 1 chai zikmu, Kol Nidre,* and more. Whenever they looked at me, they laughed. They got my goat. 1 could not stand them anymore; they made me miserable. I got up my nerve when they came around the next time. "*Frauleins,* you are laughing at me. I may not be good looking, but we are going to the land of fortune. So here is my prediction. Since I am not good looking, I will be granted good *mazel* (luck). You are pretty girls, and you will have *schwarz mazel* (bad luck)." Well, they left immediately, not returning to bother me anymore.

One morning the captain announced the ship would be docking at Ellis Island on July 4th at ten o'clock in the morning. Now more singing broke out and people took addresses from one another, planning to meet in New York as *hiffs bruder* (boat brothers). Since I was going to Boston they put a sign on me, "To Boston, South Station." July 4th arrived, and from afar we saw the Statue of Liberty. There were handshakes, hugs, tears; friends and family were waiting for the newcomers. The ship docked and everyone had to go through the Custom House, see the doctors, get vaccinations, and take care of all other formalities--"Name and address, father's name, mother's name...How much money are you bringing into this country?...Who is to take care of you until you can earn a living?" If you had any money with you, customs officers let you go through, if you had no money, someone had to be responsible for you. I was a rich man; I still had my two dollars sewn in my vest.

After a couple of hours, I was transferred to the Fall River Line going to Fall River and Boston, Massachusetts. At five o'clock in the morning the boat docked. I was taken by the HIAS organization onto a train where they gave us breakfast, an orange. In Mikulince you got an orange when you were sick. At least, however, I was on my way to Boston. The train neared South Station. Here I was, with a little satchel, carrying just underwear, a couple of shirts and pants, away from home, thousands of miles, having traveled for two weeks, without a bath, without enough to eat, and not knowing what was going to happen next. I had accomplished, with the help of my mother and father, the learning of a trade and with God's help I would be able to help myself make a living and provide for the family at home. Suddenly the train stopped. "All out, South Station, Boston." I am in America! I took my baggage, got down, walked, and walked, and walked, my heart aching for my father, my mother, brother, my friends, the family that I left behind. At the gate I noticed a very stout woman waving to me. It was my aunt, Esther Rifke Rosenberg.

My First Days in America

The Rosenbergs lived at #6 Auburn Street in the West End of Boston. Esther and Max Rosenberg as well as Dave and Jenny Appel lived in one apartment. Esther had one daughter, Bessie. I arrived at their home on a Sunday morning, July 5, 1907. 1 said the morning prayer, and we sat down at the table. It was my first breakfast in America. They served fried flounders, strawberries, cream, coffee, and scrambled eggs. I felt like crying, though, for I was actively thinking of home. Over there, people did not eat so much, even on a holiday. I started to give the relatives a report from home, under a deluge of questions. No sooner had we finished eating when the landsleit began to gather. Everyone wanted to know how his family was getting along at home. This inquiry lasted not just that first morning but a few days.

The first present I received came from Uncle Dave Appel, a pair of shoes. They were secondhand shoes with heavy soles and little metal horseshoes tapped on the heels, so the heels would not rub down so fast. On Tuesday morning, the peddler came by. The relatives started to talk with him. I had to have a suit, a *Talis* (prayer shawl), and a few shirts. The peddler's name was Mr. Lakin. Immediately I was informed that in America one did not need much money on hand to buy items that one wanted. One paid for them in installments. Every week we paid one dollar until our debt for whatever we had purchased from Mr. Lakin was paid off. Both my aunts told him that he should give me a quality suit because I knew my goods; I was a tailor. So, the next day

51

Mr. Lakin and 1 went up to Cross Street, upstairs to a wholesale clothing business. Every suit had a ticket indexed by initials, with no price listed. If one had a card from the peddler, he could take the suit. We selected a suit along with two pairs of pants. The shirts and the *Talis* will be brought to me next week. Meanwhile, I said my prayers three times a day and the prayers were good to me. Every Sunday landsleit and family would get together and play cards, usually poker. I started to get used to life in America, little by little. And I changed. The two sisters could not get along living together, so Dave and Jennie moved to Brighton Street. Since Aunt Jennie was expecting, I remained with Esther Rosenberg, and she took in a few boarders to help pay her expenses. After a couple of weeks, I had already become well dressed, with my suit, and a new haircut, so we went out to take pictures to send home.

During the third week, on a Sunday, a landsman from some city in Galicia who had a tailor store in Somerville offered me a job for three dollars a week. I accepted the offer and Uncle Max Rosenberg told me how to travel to Somerville. Carfare was five cents, one way. In the morning, my aunt Esther handed me a paper bag. In it was bread, a half pint bottle of coffee and an apple. I walked into the tailor shop and within minutes the first item I was given to make was a vest which looked just like the vests in Mikulince. Well, I felt sick, perhaps from the memories. 1 came home and told my aunt that I did not like the job. I could have done better for myself at home. Meanwhile I knew that my friend from home, Morris Kostazky, who had also come to Boston, had

52

gotten a job in a cloak factory as an assistant to a cloak operator. So, the second day of work I went back to Somerville and said to Mr. Kerner, that was the tailor's name, that I did not enjoy this type of work. He instantly offered me four dollars a week. I worked for one week, got my four dollars, took an envelope, sent home one dollar, gave Esther three dollars, and told her I would not be going to Somerville anymore. I just did not like it. Esther and I had our first blow-out, "What did you think when you came to America...*to shar gelt mit a lopato*?...That you would dig money with a shovel?" 1 started crying and could not stop.

I took a walk over to Aunt Jenny's. Uncle Dave was a Columbus tailer, a skirt maker, who was earning nine dollars a week. I told Dave I would like to be a skirt maker, too, then I cried, saying that I wanted to go home. But how could I do that? I did not have a penny. "Well," he said, "come with me tomorrow to my brother Barney's. He is a good skirt maker; he makes good money. Do not say anything. 1 will do the talking.' Dave gave me ten cents for a shave, the first shave I had. I went back to Esther's and told her I was going up town with Uncle Dave to see Barney. That next morning Barney agreed that I would start working for him as a helper, the first four weeks for nothing, then at two dollars a week for four weeks and he would keep raising me from there. I told him I was a good tailor, so he brought the terms down to three weeks for nothing and then four dollars a week. Meanwhile Esther gave me 10 cents a week spending money and 10 cents a week for a shave. I walked to work every morning from the West End of Boston to Essex Street. This

53

kind of work I enjoyed. The hours were from seven to six, Monday through Friday, and Saturday from seven to one in the summer, and seven to five in the fall. After three weeks I received an advance payment of four dollars. 1 brought it home and gave it to Esther. She still gave me only twenty cents a week.

My menu for lunch was changed to two boiled eggs and coffee. Italian fruit peddlers used to come up to the shop, so I would buy an apple or orange from the ten cents spending money. Finally, a favorable change took place. The operators in the shop began organizing a union and called a strike. After six weeks on strike, the operators lost out at their request, and they all went off for other work. I had already gotten to know some of the operators, and they offered me a job with better pay elsewhere. I told Barney I was leaving him. Then he started to talk turkey, making me a money proposition. He had taken on a contract to make all the skirts for the Metropolitan Cloak and Suit Company, and I would be his partner, a 60 and 40 proposition with him getting 60 and me getting 40 cents of each dollar. The deal was sealed. we hired six helpers: Uncle Dave at eleven dollars a week; Beryl Greenberg, 10 dollars; Rachmiel, 10 dollars; Hershel, 5 dollars per week; Leibel, 9 dollars; Jankel *der schwarzer* (a black or swarthy person), 9 dollars a week. The first Saturday after paying everyone, we were left with 140 dollars. I got 56 dollars. I went home and gave it to Esther. Week in and week out, I still got 20 cents and gave her all my earnings. She bought me another suit from Mr. Lakin and everything she said to me was prefaced with "honey" and *tdearie*".

I started to work with no time limits on the day. There were no basting machines at the time, and we had to make a voile skirt which was pleated. Barney chalk-marked the pleats, and I would come in at two in the morning and baste them by hand so that when the operators arrived at work everything was ready for them to stitch. I wanted to make more money before the holidays and Esther gave me 10 dollars to send home. I got ten wishes for every cent I sent home. The breakfasts on Sundays did not continue to be like the first Sunday breakfast I had when I came to America. Esther would buy cracked eggs and boil them, so naturally I got sick. The *landsleit* gave me whiskey *shnapps* with ginger to ease my belly pains. This problem kept on for months.

In the fall I began to go to classes at the Philips School. That is where the Phillips House of Mass. General Hospital is now, but on a back street. I got into the eighth grade immediately and was advised to go on to prep school by the principal, but my mind continued to focus on the skirts and on making money. Some weeks my pay was as much as 80-100 dollars.

One night 1 went over to Aunt Jennie's for supper and Uncle Dave said to me, "How much money do you have for yourself?" I said, "Nothing at all. 1 gave all the extra money to Esther." "*Oy Gewald*," said Dave, "I am coming over tomorrow to find out what she is doing with your money." Next day, he was there as promised and said, "Esther, why are you taking his money? Let him save it." Esther said, "He owes me a lot of money." She then took out a big book in which she kept a record from the day I had come, adding to the fare and ticket she had sent me. Pages and pages: 10 cent pieces; $2.50 a day for board from the day 1 arrived; $25 for the *Talis*; $25.00 a piece for two suits. All the things she had bought me from Lakin were listed, and even the trolley fare that she occasionally paid for me on Sundays when we went on a picnic or out to Revere Beach. So, after two nights of constant figuring, allowing for every single item, she still owed me three hundred dollars. Uncle Dave made his suggestion: deduct three dollars a week from the money you owe him to cover his expenses and let him save his money. That became the agreed upon arrangement. So that Saturday after getting my pay, I put five dollars in my pocket and opened a bank account at the Five and Ten Cents Saving Bank passbook #585949. Then I went home. Esther was in bed and had left no supper. Sc, I went to a lunchroom and got a soda and blintzes. Next morning, she felt sick again. Uncle Max gave me eggs which I could not eat. Monday she finally offered me lunch in a paper bag, a half pint of coffee and a banana. It was pouring rain and windy, fall in Boston, and I was carrying an old umbrella. When I came to Boston Commons, the umbrella tipped over and the bag dropped, the bottle breaking. I came into the shop soaking wet. At twelve o'clock the power on the machines stopped; everybody ate except for me. There was a finisher, Mania Schneider, who also worked as a contractor with his son Sam and his son-in-law Ruben as well as with a few Italians and Americans. Mania used to bring in pots filled with food that was

56

delicious. He invited me to help him out and I accepted. That was the best meal that I had had in days. I started doing the same thing, eating with them every noon time.

Meanwhile, I got to be a good friend with Sam Schneider and went out doing things with him. We went to L Street BathHouse and the Dover Street Bath Showers since our own homes had no baths and no electricity, only gas. Staying in Esther's house was pure agony. Her treatment of me was terrible, clearly because I no longer paid her. I saved my money and kept sending money home every week to my parents, the letters returning from Europe being full of blessings. My father was going to Reb Kopally in Tarnopol, and I would receive letters saying I should send the Rebby a *pidyon*, meaning a helping hand, and God would be good to me.

Day by day I grew more fed up with my Aunt Esther. So, one Sunday morning I took a walk to East Boston to visit Uncle Flaschner, the dean of the family. One had to walk to Atlantic Avenue and there take the ferry, costing one cent to cross to East Boston, then walk home. They lived at 326 Chelsea Street. When I came in, there were quite a few *landsleit* and family sitting and talking around a table, some playing poker. 1 watched the game and whispered about the best card play move. Well, I got a *flask* (slap) in my face from Louis Tunis..."In America, greenhorn, you have to be quiet." That started a small rumble, but the men kept on playing. The house there was a *kesselgarten* (mob scene) with news being gathered there from home. Aunt Chasa,

Uncle's wife, served drinks and meals. Her kids, Abe ("Jerry") and Hymie, sold the Sunday papers; Sarah, her daughter, was out working as a telephone operator, Celia was helping around the home. From then on, every Sunday I went there and joined the group. The only Sunday I did not go to East Boston was when I went riding Saturday night with my uncle Max Rosenberg delivering meat to his customers. Uncle Max was a butcher and had customers in the Cambridge and Somerville areas. So, I went along to get some fresh air, riding all night, sore from the ride. But I found it better than sleeping in a stuffed apartment with three rooms and four boarders. It was so crowded that the Rosenberg's only daughter, Bessie, a real husky girl, about six years old at that time, slept on a couch with a distant cousin, Dave Redner.

Coming to work one day without having any lunch with me, I took myself to a restaurant for the first time. Lunch cost only 15 cents from soup to nuts, but I previously had avoided going because I had been told to beware, newcomers got sick eating in restaurants. One day the old man Schneider said to me, "Itzchok Abe, why don't you move in with me? You will be in my house like home. (My home will be your home.) Sam is your age, and you can share a bed with him." It sounded like a clever idea, and I told this to Uncle Dave Appel. "Sure," he said, "why do you have to suffer?" "You can move in with me, too, if you want." This was out of the question. I had come to America where I formed a grudge against my aunts, Esther Rifke and Jenny. And they had bad feelings towards my mother in Europe. So, I decided to ask the advice of Uncle Flaschner in East Boston that Sunday. I felt on Sunday morning that I had to make a definite decision, but how was I to go about making it?

Breakfast, pancakes, and half chicory coffee were served to all the Rosenberg's boarders, Dave Redner, Rose Flaschner (now Brown), me, Malke, Yisroel, and Eiziks. After breakfast I mentioned that I was going to East Boston for the day. "Don't you want to go to the picnic with us at Norumbega Park? We are hiring a buggy. I am preparing *semoniches* (sandwiches)," Esther said. I thanked her but told Esther that I liked to watch the card playing and get reports from Europe and I had to write letters for some of the *landsleit,* to their wives and children that they left behind. Some of these *landsleit* already had sent tickets and fare for their families. There were many patterns for bringing family over. Some sent for their children before their wives and others for their wives without their children. But regardless, the station was always at Uncle Flaschner's in East Boston. I said good-bye to Esther and left, my mind set on going to Uncle's for advice for myself.

Coming in, there was as usual a full house and a pleasant atmosphere. There was always food—-*latkes* (potato pancakes), beer by the barrel full--as well as cards and an important discussion about establishing a society named the Mikulince Benefit Association. That day Uncle Flaschner became the President; Sarah the secretary; and Burach Gallner, the treasurer. They drank "*l'chaim*" ("a toast to life") and set the dues at 25 cents a month. They spoke about having a charter to be a legal organization. Then, they talked of forming a credit union, for members only, money to be borrowed at 10% interest. Ultimately, they went into real estate, buying houses on West Eagle Street in East Boston. The organization lasted a brief time, until each person wanted to be the boss; accusations flowed, and it all went to pieces and fell apart. Uncle and Jake Flaschner remained holders of the properties.

Over time, I took cash, and sent it to Sam, my brother. I also sent him carfare from our city to Hamburg, Germany, where he took the boat over. I know it was tough for my folks to have him leave and they did not expect me to send a ticket so fast. They were just testing me on the issue. It took months after receiving it for them to decide whether to let him go or to send the ticket back to me.

For board at the Schneider's 1 paid $2.50 per week, which included food, laundry, and drinks. I remember how one Saturday I came home, and Mrs. Schneider said to me, "Itzchok Abaly, I am going to ask you for a raise." That week my take home pay was 80 dollars, and they all knew it. I was a boy of 17 years making that much, whereas a married man with children, such as my Uncle Dave, might work for me and make 13 dollars a week. I thought she would ask for a large raise. I asked how much she wanted. She said I would have to give her three dollars a week, a fifty-cent raise. I soon became the idol of the house and was treated like a king.

I did not go to Esther Rifke's. Sometimes I'd go to Jenny's or

East Boston, but mainly I kept busy with the clubs and the boys. I was already considered by those who knew me to be well-off. When my new suits came back from the tailor I became a real sport--I now had a light double-breasted suit with two pairs of pants and a black single-breasted one with white stripes, two pairs of pants, and a fancy vest. Next, I bought a watch and chain. The chain weighed 14 pennies and was 14 carat gold; the watch, 17 jewels with a Waltham movement. It was in a P.S. Bartlet case, Then I went to take pictures of myself at Hoffman's on Everett Street and sent them home. When my folks in Poland got the picture, they were stunned. When I had left home, I was a small skinny, noticeably short boy, with dark hair, and side beards, and here I was now a handsome boy, taking a beautiful picture, with a watch chain in my suit.

This transformation made my brother decide to come to America. Within two months he arrived. I met him at South Station and, true to my mother's desires, brought him over to Esther Rifke's. I immediately got him two suits, shoes, and a supply of shirts to start him off. That was the first time I had been to Esther's since I had moved away. And of course, I told her that I would pay her for his board.